THE
LABRADOR THEORY

Text © 2014 Cheever Hardwick
Illustrations © Alasdair Hilleary

First published in the UK in 2014
by Quiller, an imprint of Quiller Publishing Ltd

British Library Cataloguing-in-Publication Data
A catalogue record for this book
is available from the British Library

ISBN 978 1 84689 196 0

Printed in Malta by Gutenberg Press Ltd

Quiller
An imprint of Quiller Publishing Ltd
Wykey House, Wykey, Shrewsbury, SY4 1JA
Tel: 01939 261616 Fax: 01939 261606
E-mail: info@quillerbooks.com
Website: www.quillerpublishing.com

THE
LABRADOR THEORY

by Cheever Hardwick

CARTOONS BY ALASDAIR HILLEARY

This book is dedicated to Susie, without whose love, support and gentle prodding this timeless prose would have remained the verbal ramblings of a dedicated admirer of the Labradorian character and spirit......

Contents

Preface

We have all witnessed the startling phenomenon of dogs that are a mirror of their owners. There is the Kensington WAG with her miniature poodle, both of them plucked, nipped and buffed to within an inch of their pampered lives. Or at the other end of the scale, the rat-catcher with his scruffy terrier cross-breed, both of whom look like they have been dragged backwards through the same hedge.

Dig any deeper, however, and these similarities tend to be one-dimensional and cosmetic. When we consider Labradors and their devoted owners, we enter an entirely different school of behavioral psychology. Occasionally Labradors will look like their owners, especially a bit later in life when edges begin to soften on both man and beast. However, this is just the beginning. The resemblance is more than skin deep. What I intend to show in the next few chapters is that Labradors act and think like their masters to an astonishing extent.

Or, perhaps, is it the other way round?

Now, before the Kennel Club or *Country Life* become over-excited about my findings, I should admit that my research is incomplete. To date, I have only studied the male of our own species. And that is for a very good reason… I firmly believe that by scrutinising the life cycle, habits, basic needs, advantages and flaws of our favourite retriever *(Labradoribus horizontalibus)*, the fairer sex has a much greater chance of deciphering the everyday whims and habits of the human male *(Labradoribus verticalus).*

I call this the Labrador Theory. Put simply, if you understand the dog, you will understand the master. With the help of Alasdair's splendid cartoons, I will take you on a crash course on the nature and nurture of Labradors, demonstrating just how similar and integral they are to our own human development. Presuming that I make my case strongly enough, this treatise will demand publication in *The Lancet* or at least an honourable mention in *Cosmopolitan*.

Together we will walk the shared evolutionary path from prehistoric hunter-gatherer to the modern day hunter-blatherer. We will compare and contrast those crucial formative years from birth to adolescence, when our worst habits become ingrained. We will then saunter through the glory years of headstrong manhood, the sowing of the proverbial oats and the quest for achievement. Finally we will examine the final stages of the parallel lives of man and Labrador.

As a self-help book, this latter age of man – the 'slipper'd pantaloon' as Shakespeare so eloquently put it – is undoubtedly the most pertinent. For the long-suffering wife with her worries about how to keep the marital fires burning after the pups have flown the basket, search no further; practical guidance is at hand. Likewise, for the long-toothed male seeking a peaceful life, then perhaps surreptitiously place this book on a strategic coffee table or car seat where your better half is sure to find it. If the Labrador Theory succeeds in denying just one divorce lawyer his fees, then I will consider this book to have been a most worthwhile exercise.

I sincerely hope that you will enjoy this book, and if some basic truths manage to sink in by the end, then it has all been time well spent for both author and reader. At the very least, men should take heart as they are related to the finest breed of dog on earth.

Cheever Hardwick

Chapter One

BROTHERS BENEATH THE SKIN

As we shall learn in later chapters, there is no shortage of

anecdotal evidence to support my assertion than today's

Labradors and their masters are cut from the same cloth.

But to earn the respect of fellow anthropologists (and any

Labradologists, for that matter), I must offer scientific proof

as well… or at least my version thereof.

We know that humans and dogs emerged from the same genetic swamp. In the grand scheme of things, our evolutionary journeys from the primordial soup only diverged quite recently (at some point within the Eocene epoch, fifty million years or so in the past). And despite our more obvious differences – number of legs, fur, tail, etc. – we were soon on a parallel course. Why? Because the ancestors of today's Labradors were not foolish. They worked out very quickly that if they helped track down quarry, barked at strangers and offered a sympathetic audience when their masters wanted to moan about trivialities, then they would get food, a place by the fire and affection aplenty.

Little has changed. Indeed, the unbridled gusto with which early man and his eager canine companion rushed out in the morning, leaving an angry woman and screaming infants behind, has not diminished with the passage of time.

So much of what we take for granted today sprang from those more perilous times. For example, the master needed only to put on his favourite woolly mammoth breeks and the faithful mutt would leap and squeal with excitement like an unhinged firefly by the entrance to the family cave. He instinctively knew that something exciting was afoot.

Interestingly, the human male's fascination for marking his territory on the nearest bush seems to have emerged from this era, and it is deeply embedded in the male psyche to this day. Note the relish with which both man and his canine cohort head for a leafy receptacle, a look of keen anticipation (and often desperation) etched on their faces. Yet despite the pressing need, they will often delay the moment of release until they find the perfect target.

A surreptitious pee in someone else's garden brings even more pleasure. This is especially stimulating for good old *verticalus* at one of those dreaded dinner parties, where trying to knock the petals off the roses carries an added element of danger.

James Bond, move over.

But I digress. Of course, much of my theory is difficult to prove or, hopefully, disprove. However, as the centuries turned into millennia, there is no contesting that the differing types and roles of dogs became more defined. The fast and keen-sighted ones herded livestock. The fierce and loud-mouthed guarded the home. The useless and yappy were carried around in Gucci handbags. However, it was the resourceful retriever that earned the closest relationship with man. By helping his master in his search for fresh meat, the precursor of today's Labrador assured himself of a spot close to the fire and the choicest of hand-downs from the table.

And they still do…

For anyone who struggles to understand the intense bond of camaraderie and partnership between a Labrador and its master, then allow me to offer a simple explanation. It is an integral part of our DNA, implanted over time. The human male is hard-wired this way. Naturalists and behavioral psychologists will claim that domesticated animals are innately programmed to react to certain stimuli. Well, so are domesticated men! We have no choice in the matter. Spending time in the outdoors with our favourite canine is not a hobby… it is not a luxury… it is a part of being human and male.

Chapter Two

LEARNING THE BASICS

It is hardly surprising that both *Labradoribus verticalus* and *Labradoribus horizontalibus* show many of the same characteristics, when one considers that their adolescent development is remarkably similar.

Most puppies and young boys are offered a certain level of tolerance in those early months or years before their respective noses are firmly rubbed in their mistakes. The basic lessons hopefully stay with them: sit still, stop whining, and don't cock your leg on Great Aunt Agatha's prize begonias.

Of course, there are those of both the human and canine ilk that manage to escape these early disciplines. (Or, more accurately, there are dog owners and parents who chose not to put the basic ground rules in place.) The ill-behaved scamps are disruptive at best, charging every which way, seeking attention, and generally making a nuisance of themselves. 'They need to let off a bit of steam at that age', say the unrepentant guardians of the monstrosity in question. 'He's just expressing himself.' Exactly – all over Aunt Agatha's prize begonias!

Eating habits are also similar during those formative years, on both the human and canine fronts. Every meal is gobbled and gulped as though it were the last. The respective bowls are licked to a shine, as well as any other bowl they can get their snouts into. And if it is edible – no matter how runny, ripe or fresh it may be – it still counts as food and will be ingested regardless of the consequences. Let's be honest – a sulky teenager would chew the sofa too, if he did not have to get off it first.

Schooling is another stage which is taken very seriously. Very often, the wide-eyed cherub or irrepressible puppy is sent off at great expense. They are dropped off at the imposing doors of some eminent boarding school or gamekeeper in the blind hope that the appallingly bad manners which had been allowed at home will miraculously be converted to civilised behaviour.

On a somewhat serious note, this can be a difficult stage in the development of both man and dog. Some dogs turn out to be gun-shy and some children are not best suited to fierce competition. The Drill Sergeant approach often works, but endless barracking can also break the thinner-skinned recruits. Both owners and parents may have to adapt to the realities of life and their respective charges may not turn out as originally anticipated. Other avenues will appear. The less-than-perfect retriever will be adored for other reasons.

'Alright you lot... where's the flipping partridge?'

Time and experience can bring opportunity. Once the penny has dropped that they are not top dog in all situations, most dogs and children find their feet and, to the utter astonishment of all concerned, unruly youth becomes productive adulthood. The apprehensions and disappointments of the past will hopefully become pride and admiration for the present.

Chapter Three

THE GLORY YEARS

Our high summers on this earth – the 'dog days', if you will – offer precious, never-to-be-forgotten times. This prime period of our lives can last for many happy canine years or human decades. It all depends whether your water bowl is viewed as half-full or half-empty. In this respect, both the vertical and horizontal versions of *Labradoribus* have unbounded enthusiasm for life and all of its wonders. They approach each day with wide eyes and wagging tail; both species occasionally walk into walls as a result, but it is a small price to pay.

This is a time for great feats of physical exertion (see chapters 5 and 6) and sweeping romantic gestures (see chapter 7), both of which may diminish in later years. This is the time to taste the best of what life has to offer (see chapter 8). An adventurous spirit is rewarded in these years.

Most dogs and men need to earn a crust some way or another if they want to live a comfortable and reasonably carefree existence. All too often the career paths of both are all too similar – fetching, carrying, obedience to one's master. At the start, both dog and man benefit from watching their elders, they are kept on a tight leash and are only sent out for menial tasks when there is little chance of messing them up. As novices, they will always look the part and show bags of enthusiasm, but they haven't a clue as to what's really going on. Praise is lapped up, while any rebuke is quickly shrugged off, replaced again by boundless optimism and panting ambition.

Slowly but surely, these greenhorns prove their worth. They develop their nose for business, sniffing out tasty opportunities that lie hidden in the deep grass. Of course, there are those hard-mouthed individuals who choose another path, regardless of training. They prefer the easy pickings, pinching birds they should not or mugging people in broad daylight rather than toiling through the thorns and deep water of a worthwhile career. Most seem to get away with it for years, although a few face incarceration (either thrown in the back of a Land Rover after the first drive or else at Her Majesty's Pleasure).

For those who achieve a work-life balance, the rewards are manifold. Some become lords of their patch, learning their local topography intimately. Others travel extensively, or emerge as captains of industry. To these winners come the spoils – recognition, the best food in their bowls, plenty of willing mates and their profiles in the *Financial* and/or *Shooting Times.*

All this diligence serves a long-term purpose as well. When the professional vim and vigour starts to fade, when they would rather read the paper than make the headlines, when the alarm clock no longer sends them bounding for the door – both man and Labrador have the infrastructure in place for a comfortable and happy retirement from the fray.

The 'Glory Years' don't stop… it is just that we find new priorities.

Chapter Four

THE GREY AREAS

So far, as part of my Labrador Theory, we have investigated the early and middle ages of man and his best friend, demonstrating that we both cling to this mortal coil in much the same way and for the same reasons. But I must repeat that my studies have not been done for academic satisfaction. This book has a serious social message. It offers a timely crutch for any wife who is beginning to panic because she feels that she cannot comprehend what is going on inside that rapidly greying head of her husband.

The answer is to look at his dog. Because it is true; in our later years, the lines that separate mutt and master become increasingly blurred.

Yes, it's very tempting to make the obvious jokes about their common physical challenges – weakening eyesight, unholy breath, selective hearing, failing memory, the constant need to pee, dribbling at both ends, stiffness in the morning (for the wrong reasons) – but this approach is not constructive, as most wives well know.

Confusion can creep in, however, when Lady Priscilla tries to second-guess what Sir Humphrey is thinking. Picture them at the Towers, halfway through their third gin. She is playing solitaire; he and his Labrador are standing at the window to the garden, deep in thought. The shadows are lengthening off the croquet hoops. Suddenly a peacock shrieks, the clock strikes seven, and it hits her across the face like a riding crop:

'He's bored! Utterly disinterested! Just look at him, staring into the distance… He's planning a way out, I know it… He wants to trade me in for a younger, racier model. That's it…! Maybe he already has? He went down to London twice last month… Oh Humpy, how could you? After all we have been through together…? Well, don't think I can't play you at your own sordid game. I can still turn heads at the tennis club. I'll show you…'

Before you can say deuce, their previously happy marriage has dissolved into a mess of separate beds, local gossip and awkward cocktail parties. If only she had read this book, all this unpleasantness could have been avoided. She would have known that the answer to her fears was sitting on his wagging bottom, staring out of the same window as his master, trying to spot the rabbit he had smelled earlier in the day.

Truly, she had nothing to fear… it is not a complicated formula.

Chapter Five
THE SHOOTING FIELD

Well, what was her dear husband thinking about?

There is a very high probability that he was not even
in the drawing room at that precise moment. Not
in spirit anyway. Just as his faithful Labrador was
dreaming of chasing a rabbit and bringing it back
to his master (or scoffing the lot, more likely), so his
nibs was out playing the field.

His imagination could have transported him to any number of fleshpots. Peg Three on the Home Drive, perhaps, during a south westerly at the end of November when the leaves are off the trees and the pheasants are well-feathered. The sun is twinkling on the hoar and the host cannot miss. He is in deep concentration, selecting only the most difficult birds to bring down with enviable agility. Of course, this idyllic scenario is not complete unless Bomber emerges from the blackthorns with the cock no other dog could pick.

Or maybe he's stalking Farthing Pool
on the Lower Missle as the gnats
dance across the bubbling dapple.
He had watched the brownies rise
the day before and assembled his
tackle accordingly. Now, deft as a
cat-burglar moving across the city
rooftops, he drops his nymph within
an inch of a big'un. His faithful
friend yawns on the bank behind
him, willing the fish to take.

Perhaps his internal monologue was chasing an old grouse.

'Times have changed and not for the better. When I was a lad, bah, we did things properly. There's no respect nowadays. Gun safety? They haven't got a clue, these youngsters. I'll need to get my Barbour lined with Kevlar, if I'm not careful.'

On rare occasions, Bomber does not appear in these fantasies. Daydreams of riding out with the hounds leaves little room for Labradors. However, add in a duck, goose, pheasant, partridge or next door's ginger tom, then the partnership is back in full swing.

And just as his trusty cohort would become stale and portly if he were denied the chance to chase down and retrieve quarry, so *Labridoribus verticalus* needs regular exposure to the elements in search of fin, fur or feather. He still wants to bag high-flying, expensive birds with plump breasts. However, after a good meal of venison pie and suet dumpling washed down with some decent claret, any desire for wanton seduction and lustful exertion is soon dulled by a fireside snooze or *Midsomer Murders*.

As a famous ditty
nearly said:

If a happy wife you'll be
Listen carefully to me
I can tell you for a fact
In the field, don't distract
Keep control of all your pooches
Then no need for his excuses

Chapter Six

EYE ON THE BALL

Another regular crossover between Labrador and owner
is their obsession with ball sports. Back in the mists
of time, there must have been a cylindrical creature
that rolled down hills and tasted blooming marvellous.
How else do we explain the irrepressible urge to stop
whatever's going on and fix all attention on catching,
hitting, kicking or chasing a ball?

You can carry out your own scientific experiment, if you like. Toss a tennis ball near a Labrador and there's no prize for guessing what happens next. (Don't do this on a linoleum or polished wooden floor if you value your table legs.) This 'ball reflex' will work on small boys too. Most (but not all) adults will manage to stop themselves from haring after the ball. But walk them near a telly when Wimbledon's on – or the Ashes, Masters, Six Nations or FA Cup for that matter – then you've lost them. Again, there's nothing sinister about this. If anything, it should be encouraged, especially in retirement.

Sir Humphrey, as he stood by that window, may have relived his last wicket stand with Buddy Perkins to beat the Old Carfordians. Or the time he stiffed a four iron into the breeze on the eighteenth at Pandemonium, leaving a five-footer for a birdie. Or his outrageous dummy to score under the posts in the final of the Frindle Hall Sevens. Down the years, those feats have become faster, higher and stronger as the memory of reality fades. Bomber was but a glint in his great-grandfather's eye, yet he's heard the commentary many times over.

Of course, this sporting life doesn't rely on balls. The aged squire may have slalomed down the Swiss Wall or braved the Cresta Run, as he gazed upon his garden lawn. He could have climbed the North Face or ridden a National winner. There are even those who enjoy running for the sake of it. Maybe he was sprinting past Usain Bolt or leaving Mo Farah in his wake up the home stretch.

Why does this matter? Because, a man who gets to chase balls to his heart's content, tends to have a contented heart. Denying him this natural – nay, feral – urge to play is tantamount to suffocation. Mowing the lawn or fixing shelves or drinking tea with the vicar is no substitute.

Besides, you wouldn't want him hanging round the house all day, now would you?

Chapter Seven

LOVE IS IN THE AIR

But hang on just one darn cotton-pickin' moment, I hear the bluestockings cry. It's all well and good defending the male of the species, painting him as the Angel Gabriel in plus fours. Yet, isn't it scientifically proven that men think about sex over thirty times a day? And these steamy musings don't always feature her nibs in the supporting role! While we're at it, they might continue, if you're really looking for a comparison between master and his faithful Labrador, then sex is the clincher.

Think about it. Whenever a dog (no matter his lofty pedigree) catches the scent of an attractive bitch (any port in a storm), there follows a tried and tested (and usually flawed) mating ritual. His combination of stiff-legged preening, raised hackles, flared nostrils, slobbering and simpering most often results in a well-aimed snap of the jaws from the object of his attentions. Most often, he rather dejectedly scuttles back to home territory, tail between his legs. Visit any nightclub on a Saturday night and you'll see the same sorry scene played out repeatedly.

I'm not going to deny that some gentlemen do stray, especially in their fertile minds which house a powerful image bank of lingerie models, Swedish au pairs and other wanderlusts. Yes, there is an outside chance that Sir Humphrey was contemplating a quick grapple in the hayloft with that Mrs Puddock from the village who delivers eggs every second Tuesday in her see-through blouse. But is he actually going to act on these impulses?

Not with his hip.

Besides, I do think the Labrador Theory gathers strength when it comes to matters of the heart. Forgive me if this starts to sound soppy, but Labradors are perhaps the most loving creatures on the planet. Note the doe-eyed expression of unquestioning devotion and the yelps of unbridled joy as you return from even the shortest trip away. Or that willingness to please, as you search for ducks in a freezing pond. Now picture the stiff old warrior – his back end failing, muzzle white as snow – hunched by the Land Rover on a shoot day morning, offering his services to the last breath. That's love. Pure and simple.

The Labrador owner is likewise prone to touching displays of loyalty and affection. Perhaps the goodly squire was planning Her Ladyship's birthday, as he stared out the window:

'Round number this year… Better push the boat out… All the usual trimmings: flowers, bubbly, her favourite chocs… But then something to wow the old girl… Knock her socks off… Think, Humphrey, think… Oh, I know. Got it. Where's that LP of French love songs we used to dance to in Paris before the blasted children arrived? Somewhere in the attic… Yes, she'd love that… Candles, moonlight, a bit of Charles Aznavour… Humpy, you old tiger, you've still got it!'

Chapter Eight

CREATURE COMFORTS

Working out the male psyche (especially that of the older gentleman) really isn't too difficult to do, once you know how. The trick is to remember that men – much like their Labradors – need to feel special. We thrive on praise and a bit of affection. Without regular achievement, and suitable reward, we become crabby and subdued. In more youthful surroundings, we required showy conquests to quench our thirst for fulfilment. Perhaps a flash sports car, a 200% bonus or an Austrian ski instructress called Jana who could yodel Edelweiss, whilst back-flipping down the Hahnenkamm.

That all seems a long time ago. A hybrid Volvo now whispers where the Triumph roared. The bonuses went on school fees. And Jana still lives in Kitzbühel with thirteen grandchildren who have never heard of Julie Andrews. But while our targets shrink, the need to succeed on a daily basis stays as strong as ever. And this is where we can learn from our faithful four-legged friends.

How often do you find yourself saying 'good dog, who's a good dog?' in a silly voice when the beneficiary has done very little to earn it? A solid retrieve – whether a cock pheasant or the morning paper – merits a stroke on the ears or even a tummy tickle. That evening, he feels (and, more importantly, you feel) that he really deserves his bowl of meaty chunks and roast beef gravy.

Of course, there's nothing at all wrong with this. And (you can guess what's coming next) if you treat your husband exactly the same way – with praise and rewards – he won't wander far. In fact, he'll be curled up in your communal basket every night, waiting for you with open arms.

Let's start with praise. Tomorrow, take an active interest in those simple achievements that you may write off as 'everyday' or even 'trivial'. They convey a huge amount of pleasure and satisfaction. It could be pocketing the pot in the nine-hole scramble. Or finishing *The Telegraph* short crossword and Sudoku before lunchtime. Or giving that grey squirrel in the beeches 'the fright of his life' with the .22. 'He'll think twice before coming back' is a cue to put the kettle on and dole out teatime medals (chocolate digestives), not roll your eyes and telephone the gamekeeper.

Labradors are a busy, inquisitive breed. They're go-getters. Self-motivators. So are their owners. Friedrich Nietzsche once argued that the Superman is the exception to the rule. Not in the world of Labradors! All Labs and their owners feel that they have superpowers, well beyond the age when they should know better.

For example, a Labrador fully expects to chase down a muntjac with a thirty-yard start. He thinks he's invisible when stealing the last cookie from the coffee table. He can speak to the moon. Likewise, the mature hunter-gatherer still backs himself to shoot straight, cast far and spot a teal from a widgeon on a twilight flight. In fairness, the chances are he can and will, most of the time.

Indeed, on a driven shoot, the combination of aged gun with aged gundog can prove mightily efficient. Not for him those back-wrenching 'Archangels' above the treetops. Yet, he fills his share of the bag with neatness and style. His steady old dog also takes the easier pickings that lie closer to the peg. Together, they mop up quickly, securing two rounds of sloe gin and pork pie at elevenses.

Admittedly, there is a slight drawback to the Superman complex. Now, (and I'm putting my faith in the advertising campaigns of L'Oréal and Nivea when I say this) it seems that some women have an unhealthy obsession with wrinkles and stretch marks and rogue follicles. Even the most lovely of ladies can apparently find fault with their own physique. *Labradoribus verticalus* has no such qualms. Our fearless hero will disregard the evidence, imagining himself as taut and as handsome as ever before.

But don't worry. Just as your Lab greets his evening meal with the gusto of an Italian politician at his mother's rigatoni, so food and drink is the key to securing your husband's long-term happiness (and continued presence). Both dog and man are creatures of habit and comfort. They will not forego good food, plentiful drink and a cosy setting. They have marked their territory and are ready to defend it at all costs.

Offering up a rare fillet steak with Jersey Royals, fresh garden peas and a large glass of Chateau Pavie is no different to saying 'good dog, who's a good dog?' in a silly voice, whilst ruffling his ears. (Of course, in cooking a delicious meal you're also saying 'Hello, Darling' and 'Thanks for sticking around' and 'I love you' and all the other things we're supposed to leave to the Continentals.) By carbo-loading the old boy every night and ensuring he's pie-eyed with claret, the chances of him chasing a meaningless dalliance is vastly reduced. Besides, you're the only one who gets his jokes anymore.

There lies the paradox. Put him on a short leash, and he'll pull your arm off. Tie him down, and he'll gnaw his way free. But remove the choker, and he'll walk by your side like a pet lamb. Dog trainers rely on different methods for success. Some reach for the stick, others the carrot. Wives will make their own choices. But according to my studies, it should be the carrot every time. Mark my words. Praise and reward. Praise and reward. He'll not wander far.

Chapter Nine
THE THEORY PROVED

Bomber has enjoyed a full and contented life. As he looks back across fourteen long years from the comfort of his wicker basket by the AGA, his grey muzzle raises into a smile.

No question, his eyesight is duller than before. The days when he could mark a red-leg in dead bracken from fifty yards are behind him. But his nose is as sharp as ever. He'd find it all the same. Mobility is a growing concern. The Boss has to help him into the back of the Land Rover now, which is mildly embarrassing. But he can still pull his weight at the shoot, once he gets loose. He'll teach those young

bounders a thing or two yet.

Bomber was like them once. Flashing about, making

everything his business, head strong to a fault.

Oh, but there were some good days!

Like the time he won

the Retriever

Championships

at Windsor Castle

and had his picture

on the front of The

Field. Sir Humphrey

couldn't stop hugging him. He kept saying 'you're going to make us a mint', whatever that meant. Bomber got lots of visitors afterwards. That was fun. Heaven knows how many of his progeny are dotted across the country.

Those middle years were hard work, right enough. Different shoots, different quarry, all weathers. Four, five, six days a week during the season – the butcher's dog had nothing on him. Always by his master's side, desperate to please, never on a lead. The evenings were the best – a good towel down, a big feed, then asleep in seconds. He wouldn't swap those memories for all the geese in China.

Admittedly, he hadn't always been an angel. As a pup, he'd

shredded ten yards of silk that were meant for new curtains

in the sitting room. What did they expect? It was covered in

pheasants! Or the curious incident of the dog in the night-time,

when a whole plum pudding went missing from the larder on

Christmas Eve.

Only once was

he truly in the

doghouse. A sorry

saga, two summers ago.

Bluebell was her name. A spritely

poodle from The Gables. There was nothing Standard about her! Of course, the finger of suspicion fell on Bomber when six Labradoodle puppies arrived unexpected. But it wasn't him. Scout's honour. He'd never left the garden (more's the pity). Probably that Digger from the Bull & Bell. He was always absent without leave. Still, Bomber got the blame. He woke up in the vet's one afternoon and there was something missing. Well, two things to be precise.

But, no, he has no complaints. After all, why would he want to leave a loving home where he is top dog? His meals arrive on time. His water bowl is always full. Twice a day, he takes his master for a walk, finding new smells and old, greeting the same faces. 'Sniff and let sniff', that's his motto. Whoever says that 'familiarity breeds contempt' needs to calm down and take a leaf out of Bomber's diary.

Time for your nap, my friend. The head grows heavy, the eyes droop, a paw twitches, and he's off. For in his dreams, Bomber is still the mighty wolf. There's no rabbit he can't catch, no bitch he can't sire, no bowl he can't empty, no tree he can't sprinkle. There's a bit of life in the old dog yet!

Just like his owner, the Labrador is a special breed, conditioned to be a marvellous companion – loyal, affectionate and blessed with surprising levels of common sense. They are easily trained and will do everything within their power to please, as long as they are treated with love and affection, and reprimanded gently when absolutely necessary.

The evidence that man and his Labrador are one and the same is, I believe, overwhelming. It's possible that my Labrador Theory will court controversy in the libraries and lecture halls of academia. Bring it on, I say! The subject matter may be less lofty than those broached by Copernicus, Galileo and Darwin, but I am equally willing to back my convictions.

History will prove me right.

More importantly, though, I hope that this book will be a reminder to other halves everywhere that their man – just like their dog – is worth giving the benefit of the doubt. If he seems fidgety, grumpy or listless, then it's nothing that a strong dose of exercise, a bit of TLC, good grub and grog won't remedy.

We really are that predictable.